PUFFIN BOOKS
UK | USA | Canada | Ireland | Australia
India | New Zealand | South Africa

Puffin Books is part of the Penguin Random House group of companies
whose addresses can be found at global.penguinrandomhouse.com.

www.penguin.co.uk
www.puffin.co.uk
www.ladybird.co.uk

First published 2017
004

Written by Daniel Roy

Printed in China

A CIP catalogue record for this book is available from the British Library

ISBN: 978–0–141–36992–1

All correspondence to:
Puffin Books
Penguin Random House Children's
80 Strand, London WC2R 0RL

HARDMODE
SURVIVAL HANDBOOK

PUFFIN

INTRODUCTION

GETTING THE HANG OF TERRARIA, ADVENTURER? TIME FOR A *REAL* CHALLENGE!
Your friend the Guide might know a thing or two about the world of Terraria, but there are wonders and challenges out there that even he doesn't fully understand. That's where I, the Wizard, come in!

I will guide you through the thrills and perils known as Hardmode. But be warned: Hardmode is not for the faint of heart! Are you ready to enter the forbidden Jungle Temple, or call the Moon Lord himself down from the heavens? I can tell you all about that and more!

Prepare yourself for riches beyond compare and for mind-boggling terrors . . . Exciting, isn't it?

BEGINNER TIP

New to Terraria? Start with *Terraria: The Ultimate Survival Handbook*, available at your local bookshop or online retailer. If you like building, you will also enjoy *Terraria: Crafting and Construction Handbook*, or check out *Terraria: Exploration and Adventure Handbook* if you're in the mood for an adventure.

CONTENTS

HELPERS

Your friends and allies insisted I let them share some wisdom of their own from time to time. Just play along, will you? I know everything, of course, but they really wanna help.

CHAPTER ONE:
WHAT IS HARDMODE, ANYWAY?

There's a reason it's called *Hard* mode.

Do you miss the good old days of Terraria, when every chest could contain a life-changing treasure and you had to make it home by nightfall or the zombies would eat you? Well, you're in luck!

Everything changes when you unlock Hardmode. The world becomes a dangerous place once again, as new monsters will make short work of you. And there's no going back!

Why unlock Hardmode, then? There are a few good reasons . . .

NEW TREASURE!

Is your Molten Armor set going out of fashion? Do you wish you could fly halfway across the world? How about having weapons so powerful you can beat the Eye of Cthulhu in seconds?

Terraria becomes a much tougher place when you unlock Hardmode, but you'll also find plenty of weapons to meet the challenge.

The cat-firing Meowmere – one of the many awesome new weapons in Hardmode

NEW CRAFTS!

If you love crafting and construction, you're in for a treat! There are eleven new crafting stations available, with hundreds of great new items and building materials at your disposal. Flip to **Chapter Six: Hardmode Crafting** on page 47 for the lowdown.

New Hardmode crafting stations

Chlorophyte, one of the most powerful ores in the game

NEW ORES!

You like mining? Who doesn't! Hardmode offers you a whole bunch of new ores to swing at with your pickaxe. You can now mine exciting ores including **Cobalt**, **Mythril** and **Adamantite**. Once you complete a few challenges, you can go looking for precious **Chlorophyte** in the Underground Jungle.

NEW TOOLS!

From painting tools to mining equipment, Hardmode offers new ways to get things done. The new **pickaxes**, **axes** and **hammers** are faster and more powerful than ever. Gather enough ores and you might even manage to craft the super-exciting **Drill Containment Unit**, a Drill Mount so powerful it can clear a whole area in seconds!

The Drill Containment Unit in action

NEW ALLIES!

Not everything in Hardmode is out to kill you. You'll also get the chance to make new friends! There are seven new allies waiting for you . . . including me! You can even get a visit from Santa Claus himself during the festive season. Want to learn more? Turn to **Chapter Five: Hardmode Allies** on page 38!

NEW BIOMES!

You'll notice a big change to your biomes the second you unlock Hardmode. The **Hallow** - a deadly biome filled with pixies and unicorns - will slowly spread, while the **Corruption**, or the **Crimson**, will extend to the deepest reaches of your world.

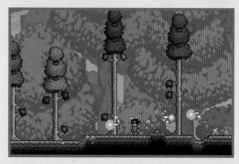

The Hallow: cuter than the Corruption, but just as deadly

NEW MONSTERS!

Up for a challenge? In Hardmode, even the familiar biomes become home to all-new deadly monsters that drop cool treasure.

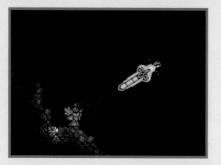

An Enchanted Sword, one of the many, many new monsters out to get you in Hardmode

NEW BOSSES!

Hardmode features new bosses who will test your reflexes and keep you on your toes. Some, like the **Twins**, **Skeletron Prime** and the **Destroyer**, are familiar foes outfitted with deadly upgrades, while others like **Plantera** or **Golem** offer entirely new fights. Get ready for an exciting challenge! For details, flip to **Chapter Seven: Hardmode Bosses** on page 57.

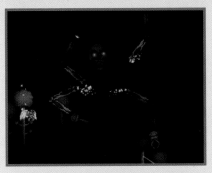

Skeletron Prime gets some serious new hardware

NEW EVENTS!

If you enjoyed defeating the Goblin Army, or facing off against bloodthirsty zombies during the Blood Moon, you're in for a treat in Hardmode: there are six new events to keep you on the edge of your seat. Turn to **Chapter Eight: Hardmode Events** on page 63 for more.

The Martians are coming! A giant UFO launches an attack during the Martian Madness event.

NEW . . . FISH?

The Angler insisted I include this one. He asked me to tell you all about fishing in lava with the **Hotline Fishing Hook**, and how he has a few exciting new quest rewards for you. If you like fishing, know that you have a few new catches to look forward to!

The Pigron Mount, only available by fishing in Hardmode

CHAPTER TWO: PREPARATIONS

TIME TO GEAR UP!

In the first few days, Hardmode can be a pretty deadly place. Here are a few things you can do beforehand to make it a little less fatal.

You don't have to do all of these things before you enter Hardmode, but they'll definitely make your life easier. It is also possible to perform these tasks once you've entered Hardmode, but the new monsters will make it more challenging to do so.

HELPFUL HACK

One way to access pre-Hardmode items later is to create a new world at the World Selection screen. When you need something that's too hard to get in your Hardmode world, just jump to your pre-Hardmode world and gather what you need!

HARDMODE PREPARATION CHECKLIST

DONE?	
CONSTRUCTION PROJECTS	
	Dig a Hellevator
	Prepare a boss arena
	Upgrade your base defences
CRAFTING PROJECTS	
	Upgrade your armour
	Upgrade your weapons
	Gather your minions
	Upgrade your pickaxe
	Craft an Obsidian Shield
	Craft a Mana Flower
	Upgrade your grappling hook
	Craft Frostspark Boots
	Craft any Horseshoe Balloon
	Collect some Healing Potions
	Craft some Mana Potions
	Craft Ironskin Potions
	Craft Regeneration Potions
	Craft Spelunker Potions

DONE?	
USEFUL ITEMS	
	Gather some seeds
	Collect buff furniture items
OTHER PREPARATIONS	
	Raise your maximum Health to 400
	Raise your maximum mana to 200
	Spot some Evil Altars
	Create a Surface Mushroom biome
	Fish for some Fishing Crates
	Craft with four Chains and one Life Crystal

BUILD USEFUL STRUCTURES

These simple construction projects will make your life in Hardmode easier in the long run.

BOTTOMING OUT: HELLEVATOR

You might want to visit the Underworld to beat the Wall of Flesh and collect some extra treasure once in Hardmode. That's where a Hellevator comes in handy! Just dig a shaft straight down until you hit the Underworld. Make sure you have **Spectre Boots**, **Cloud in a Bottle** or equivalent to avoid fall damage, and a **Magic Mirror** or an **Ice Mirror** to get back to the surface again.

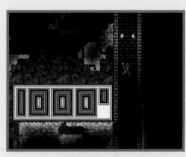

Going down!

READY TO RUMBLE: BOSS ARENA

The bosses you'll face in Hardmode require a lot of space to manoeuvre around, so building an arena is a sure-fire strategy for success. Place your arena away from your base, and layer **platforms** on top of one other, just high enough to jump between. Make your arena at least one screen wide, or even wider.

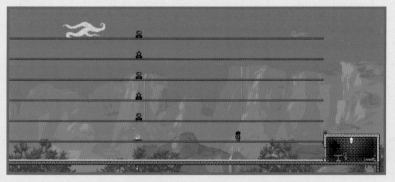

A simple arena with honey and housing for the Nurse

Useful things to put around your arena include **Heart** and **Star Statues** (wired to a **5 Second Timer**), **honey**, **Heart Lanterns** and **campfires**. You can even build a house for the Nurse so you can have her nearby!

IT'S A TRAP: BASE DEFENCE

Your run-of-the-mill zombie doesn't have enough of its brain left to open a door, but the monsters you'll face in Hardmode events certainly know how to turn a doorknob. Us allies can hold our own against a stray monster or two, but if you don't want us to die every time the pirates or the Martians show up, upgrade your base defences!

One great way to defend your base is to place walls wired with **actuators** at the entrance. This way, you'll only have to deal with the monsters who can fly through walls. You can also use **lava** or **dart traps** to deadly effect.

The entrance to an underground bunker base. Looks innocent enough . . .

. . . until you turn it into a death trap!

SURVIVAL TIP

Always keep my house in an accessible spot. Trust me, you'll want your friendly Nurse nearby when the invaders come knocking!

UPGRADE YOUR ARMOUR

Make sure you have the best armour you can get! This is one of the most important things to do before entering Hardmode, as monsters will deal a lot more damage than you're used to. Choosing which set of armour you should make depends on your playing style.

TIN CANNED: MOLTEN ARMOR

Like to get up close and personal with enemies? Consider a set of Molten Armor. This armour has the highest pre-Hardmode Defense and gives you a nice bonus on your melee attacks. If you're not sure what set to get, pick this one.

RECIPE	INGREDIENTS	CRAFTING STATION
Molten Helmet (1)	Hellstone Bar (10)	
Molten Breastplate (1)	Hellstone Bar (20)	Iron/Lead Anvil
Molten Greaves (1)	Hellstone Bar (15)	

DEAD SERIOUS: NECRO ARMOR

Do you prefer to dodge enemies and pepper them with arrows from a distance? Craft yourself some Necro Armor. Each item gives a boost to your ranged-weapon damage, and by wearing the whole set you'll consume twenty per cent less ammo.

RECIPE	INGREDIENTS	CRAFTING STATION
Necro Helmet (1)	Cobweb (40) Bone (40)	
Necro Breastplate (1)	Cobweb (50) Bone (60)	Work Bench
Necro Greaves (1)	Cobweb (45) Bone (50)	

GUERRILLA TACTICS: JUNGLE ARMOR

If you're the wizard type, then yay for you! Get yourself a set of Jungle Armor, my young apprentice. It's perfect for magic attacks that require mana to work. The set raises your maximum mana, increases the chances of your magic attacks causing critical damage, and reduces your overall mana usage. Just make sure to dodge!

RECIPE	INGREDIENTS	CRAFTING STATION
Jungle Hat (1)	Jungle Spores (8)	
Jungle Shirt (1)	Jungle Spores (16) Stinger (10)	Iron/Lead Anvil
Jungle Pants (1)	Jungle Spores (8) Vine (2)	

GET BUZZY: BEE ARMOR

If you're the queen-bee type who prefers to leave the dirty work to the worker drones, get yourself a set of Bee Armor. This set increases the number of minions you can control, and boosts their damage. Summoned minions aren't very powerful at the beginning of Hardmode, though, so grab another set such as Molten Armor too; your Bee Armor will come in handy soon enough.

RECIPE	INGREDIENTS	CRAFTING STATION
Bee Headgear (1)	Bee Wax (8)	
Bee Breastplate (1)	Bee Wax (12)	Iron/Lead Anvil
Bee Greaves (1)	Bee Wax (10)	

UPGRADE YOUR WEAPONS

Just like armour, the type of weapons you should get in preparation for Hardmode depends on how you like to play. Here are my personal recommendations:

THE FINAL CUT: NIGHT'S EDGE

Night's Edge is easily the most powerful weapon pre-Hardmode, but crafting it requires a bit of patience. To learn more about Night's Edge, flip to page 39 of *Terraria: Crafting and Construction Handbook*.

RECIPE	INGREDIENTS	CRAFTING STATION
Night's Edge (1)	Fiery Greatsword (1) Muramasa (1) Blade of Grass (1) Light's Bane* (1)	Demon/Crimson Altar

*Can be replaced with Blood Butcherer

RETURNING FIRE: CASCADE

If yo-yos are more your style, make sure to grab a Cascade! This bad boy is the strongest yo-yo before Hardmode, and has a chance of setting enemies on fire with every hit. They drop from monsters in the Underworld once you beat **Skeletron**.

FIRE AT WILL: RANGED WEAPONS

For sheer firepower, consider crafting a
Phoenix Blaster. You'll need a **handgun** to
craft it, which you can find in the Dungeon's
Golden Chests.

RECIPE	INGREDIENTS	CRAFTING STATION
 Phoenix Blaster (1)	Handgun (1) Hellstone Bar (10)	🪓 🪓 Iron/Lead Anvil

Two other great ranged weapons are the **Hellwing Bow** and the **Bee's Knees**. You can
find the Hellwing Bow in the Underworld's Shadow Chests, while the Bee's Knees drops
from the **Queen Bee**.

FEEL THE BURN: MAGIC WEAPONS

If you're smart like me and favour the magical arts, then you
have a number of great magic weapons to choose from. The
Water Bolt and the **Demon Scythe** are two of my favourites.
You can find the Water Bolt on one of the Dungeon's many
bookshelves: look for a blue book with a yellow band.

The Water Bolt on a Dungeon shelf

As for the Demon Scythe, you'll
need to pry one from the hands of
a **demon** or **Voodoo Demon** in the
Underworld. Just make sure not to
kill that Voodoo Demon over lava,
unless you want the Wall of Flesh to
make a surprise appearance!

GATHER YOUR MINIONS

Regardless of your fighting style, having an **Imp Staff** on hand is always a good idea to boost your damage. You can use it to summon an imp that will pierce multiple enemies and even set them on fire!

Make sure to use a **Bewitching Table** before heading into battle, as it will let you summon one extra imp. You can find the Bewitching Table in the Dungeon.

RECIPE	INGREDIENTS	CRAFTING STATION
Imp Staff (1)	Hellstone Bar (17)	Iron/Lead Anvil

COMBAT TIP

Once you enter Hardmode, make sure to upgrade your Imp Staff with a **Spider Staff**, crafted from **Spider Fangs**. Later, you can also get upgrades like the **Deadly Sphere Staff** from **Deadly Spheres** during a solar eclipse, **Optic Staff** from the **Twins**, and more!

UPGRADE YOUR PICKAXE

The **Molten Pickaxe** is definitely worth crafting, as you can use it to mine one of two Hardmode ores, depending on your world: Cobalt or Palladium. Not only that, it also emits light and can set your enemies on fire.

RECIPE	INGREDIENTS	CRAFTING STATION
Molten Pickaxe (1)	Hellstone Bar (20)	Iron/Lead Anvil

FISHING TIP

The Molten Pickaxe isn't the only pre-Hardmode pickaxe that can mine Cobalt and Palladium; there's the **Reaver Shark** as well! In fact, the Reaver Shark is the faster of the two. You have a small chance of catching one every time you fish in the Ocean.

CRAFT USEFUL ITEMS

The following items will make your life easier and are well worth the trouble of acquiring them before Hardmode.

HOLD STEADY: OBSIDIAN SHIELD

The Obsidian Shield will protect you against a leading cause of death for Terraria adventurers: getting knocked off a cliff. It also protects you against fire damage from Hellstone and Meteorite.

You can find the Cobalt Shield in the Dungeon's **Gold Chests** and **Golden Lock Boxes**.

RECIPE	INGREDIENTS	CRAFTING STATION
Obsidian Skull (1)	Obsidian (20)	Furnace

RECIPE	INGREDIENTS	CRAFTING STATION
Obsidian Shield (1)	Cobalt Shield (1) Obsidian Skull (1)	Tinkerer's Workshop

IT'S A KIND OF MAGIC: MANA FLOWER

This useful item belongs in the inventory of any serious magic user. I've got three myself! Equipped with a Mana Flower, you'll automatically drink Mana Potions when your mana gets too low. Not only that, but it also reduces your mana usage! Just like using Mana Potions normally, however, drinking them automatically will cause **Mana Sickness**, reducing your magic damage for five seconds.

You can find **Nature's Gift** by slashing grass in the Underground Jungle. Nature's Gift also contributes to lower mana usage, so grab two while you're there!

RECIPE	INGREDIENTS	CRAFTING STATION
Mana Flower (1)	Mana Potion (1) Nature's Gift (1)	Tinkerer's Workshop

WHIP IT REAL GOOD: IVY WHIP

As you surely know by now, a grappling hook is an essential tool for any serious adventurer. This is twice as true in Hardmode, so be sure to get the best hook available. The Ivy Whip is a great choice since it allows you to shoot three hooks at once that can reach up to twenty-five tiles.

RECIPE	INGREDIENTS	CRAFTING STATION
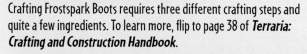 Ivy Whip (1)	Vine (3) Jungle Spores (12)	Iron/Lead Anvil

COOL RUNNINGS: FROSTSPARK BOOTS

These super-useful boots will do wonders for your speed. Not only do they let you run faster, but they also give you more mobility on ice and let you fly around like **Rocket Boots** do.

Crafting Frostspark Boots requires three different crafting steps and quite a few ingredients. To learn more, flip to page 38 of *Terraria: Crafting and Construction Handbook*.

RECIPE	INGREDIENTS	CRAFTING STATION
Spectre Boots (1)	Rocket Boots (1) Hermes Boots* (1)	Tinkerer's Workshop

*Can also use Flurry Boots or Sailfish Boots.

RECIPE	INGREDIENTS	CRAFTING STATION
Lightning Boots (1)	Spectre Boots (1) Anklet of the Wind (1) Aglet (1)	Tinkerer's Workshop

RECIPE	INGREDIENTS	CRAFTING STATION
Frostspark Boots (1)	Lightning Boots (1) Ice Skates (1)	Tinkerer's Workshop

FLOATING AWAY: HORSESHOE BALLOONS

How would you like not to die when you fall from places up high? Craft yourself a Horseshoe Balloon and you'll be all set! These items also let you jump higher and double-jump at will.

There are five types of Horseshoe Balloons you can craft depending on the ingredient you use: **Blue, Green, Pink, White** or **Yellow Horseshoe Balloons.**

RECIPE	INGREDIENTS	CRAFTING STATION
Horseshoe Balloon (1)	Any balloon (1) Lucky Horseshoe (1)	Tinkerer's Workshop

All Horseshoe Balloons require a **Lucky Horseshoe**, and all except the Pink Horseshoe Balloon require a **Shiny Red Balloon**. You can find these two items in **Floating Island Chests** or from fishing for **Sky Crates**.

BALLOON	INGREDIENTS
Cloud in a Balloon	Cloud in a Bottle Shiny Red Balloon
Fart in a Balloon	Fart in a Jar* Shiny Red Balloon
Sharkron Balloon	Tsunami in a Bottle Balloon Pufferfish
Blizzard in a Balloon	Blizzard in a Bottle Shiny Red Balloon
Sandstorm in a Balloon	Sandstorm in a Bottle Shiny Red Balloon

*Created by combining Cloud in a Bottle and Whoopie Cushion

STAY HEALTHY: HEALING POTIONS

You'll need plenty of Healing Potions – say, fifty – to survive early Hardmode. You'll find a bunch of them in **pots** in the Underground, and the Wall of Flesh also drops a few. The most reliable method, however, is to craft them yourself. Begin by crafting **Lesser Healing Potions**, then upgrade them to Healing Potions.

RECIPE	INGREDIENTS	CRAFTING STATION
Lesser Healing Potion (2)	Mushroom (1) Gel (2) Bottle (2)	Placed Bottle

RECIPE	INGREDIENTS	CRAFTING STATION
Healing Potion (1)	Lesser Healing Potion (2) Glowing Mushroom (1)	Placed Bottle

FISHING TIP

Know what's even better than Healing Potions? **Honeyfins**! These fish will restore 120 of your Health, which is twenty more than Healing Potions do. Find a **beehive** in the Underground Jungle and cast your line in honey!

BOTTOMS UP: MANA POTIONS

If you plan to use magic weapons a lot, you'd better get yourself a few Mana Potions. You can buy the **Lesser Mana Potions** you need from the Merchant for 1 Silver apiece, or look for them in the Dungeon.

RECIPE	INGREDIENTS	CRAFTING STATION
Mana Potion (1)	Lesser Mana Potion (2) Glowing Mushroom (1)	Placed Bottle

TOUGHEN UP: IRONSKIN POTIONS

This useful potion can make the difference between winning and dying in a boss fight, as it raises your Defense by eight. Make sure to craft a few stacks.

RECIPE	INGREDIENTS	CRAFTING STATION	
Ironskin Potion (1)	Bottled Water (1) Daybloom (1) Iron/Lead Ore (1)	Placed Bottle	Alchemy Table

HEALING FACTOR: REGENERATION POTIONS

Another great potion to have handy in a fight, the Regeneration Potion heals two Health points per second for five minutes. This buff will work even if you have a **Band of Regeneration** equipped.

RECIPE	INGREDIENTS	CRAFTING STATION	
Regeneration Potion (1)	Bottled Water (1) Daybloom (1) Mushroom (1)	Placed Bottle	Alchemy Table

CAVE DIVING: SPELUNKER POTIONS

One of your main challenges in Hardmode will be to find and collect resources before the monsters get to you. This super-useful potion will highlight nearby ores, gems, herbs and other treasures for five minutes. Make sure to always have a stack on hand before you head out!

RECIPE	INGREDIENTS	CRAFTING STATION	
Spelunker Potion (1)	Bottled Water (1) Blinkroot (1) Moonglow (1) Gold/Platinum Ore (1)	Placed Bottle	Alchemy Table

GATHER SEEDS

Wandering around for **herbs** is about to get much more difficult! Gather a bunch of seeds so you can plant them in the safety of your base.

Make sure you also pick a few **Mushroom Grass Seeds** from an Underground Mushroom biome. You'll need them to make a **Surface Mushroom biome**. To find out why, flip ahead to page 40 for the section on the **Truffle**.

GARDENING TIP

No need to plant your seeds outside! Craft some **clay pots** using Clay Blocks and a forge, or, better yet, buy some **planter boxes** from me.

COLLECT BUFF FURNITURE ITEMS

A few items in the game can give your combat abilities a much-needed boost. Make sure to gather the ones that fit with your combat style! Simply place them on the ground and **right-click** on them to get a temporary buff.

ITEM	BUFF	WHERE TO GET IT
Alchemy Table	Thirty-three per cent chance not to use up ingredients.	Found in Dungeon
Ammo Box	Twenty per cent chance not to consume ammo	Sold by Traveling Merchant
Bewitching Table	Allows you to have more one more minion	Found in Dungeon
Sharpening Station	Increases armour penetration	Found in the Jungle's Underground Cabins

RAISE YOUR HEALTH

You should have 400 Health before you enter Hardmode, as it will greatly increase your odds of staying alive.

Explore the Underground and Cavern layers until you locate **Crystal Hearts**. Break them with your pickaxe to get **Life Crystals**, then use these crystals to raise your Health by twenty points at a time. Repeat until you reach 400 Health.

A Crystal Heart

If you find extra Life Crystals, hold on to them! You can use them to craft **Heart Lanterns**, which you can place to increase your Health regeneration in combat.

RAISE YOUR MANA

Raising your mana to 200 is a great idea even if you don't think that magic is the best thing in the world (but that isn't you, right?). Just gather **Fallen Stars** at night and craft them into **Mana Crystals**. Each Mana Crystal will raise your maximum mana by twenty points up to a maximum of 200.

RECIPE	INGREDIENTS	CRAFTING STATION
Mana Crystal (1)	Fallen Star (3)	By Hand

OTHER PREPARATIONS

Almost done! Just a few more things to do before we get started . . .

THE EVIL YOU KNOW: LOCATE EVIL ALTARS

Demon Altars or **Crimson Altars** play a crucial role in Hardmode, as they are the key to releasing all-new ores. To save time and energy later on, take the time now to spot where your world's Evil Altars are located and make sure you can reach them easily from the surface.

Three Crimson Altars close together on a Crimson world

Figure out which altar is the closest to your base and make a note of it. Whatever you do once you enter Hardmode, do not destroy that altar! You might need it if you ever fancy crafting an item to summon one of the pre-Hardmode bosses.

OUT IN THE OPEN: SURFACE MUSHROOM BIOME

This is not absolutely necessary, but to save time in Hardmode you might want to create your Surface Mushroom biome right away, then build a house in it. If no other ally is occupying that house, the Truffle will move in as soon as you unlock Hardmode. For details on how to create a Surface Mushroom biome, flip ahead to page 41.

SUNKEN TREASURE: FISHING CRATES

You really don't have to do this one, but the Angler swears by it. If you don't want to destroy Evil Altars in Hardmode and spread corruption around your world, there's another method to gather Hardmode ore: fish for Fishing Crates. But don't open them right away! Wait until Hardmode, then check their contents. Many of them should contain Hardmode ores.

Fishing Crates: Got one!

FISHING TIP

If you want to catch Fishing Crates faster, use **Crate Potions**! These raise your chances of catching a crate by ten per cent. You can craft these using **Bottled Water**, **Amber**, **Deathweed** and **Moonglow**, or you can get them as rewards in my amazing fishing quests.

CHAPTER THREE: UNLOCKING HARDMODE

FACING THE WALL OF FLESH

**Ready for Hardmode? Even unlocking it is not going to be easy ...
Lucky I'm here to help!**

FINAL PREPARATIONS

HIGHWAY TO HELL

Once you summon the Wall of Flesh, it will move across the Underworld with nothing
to stop it. And, because the last thing you need when fighting this monstrosity is to fall
into lava, your best bet is to build one long path across the Underworld.

House in the way? Go right through it!

Build a long, straight path of at least 1000 blocks, using whatever you have to hand,
and clear everything as you go so that you have room to move. If you've got them,
set up **Heart Statues** and **Star Statues** along the way and connect them with **wire**
to a **5 Second Timer**. You can also place **campfires** and **Heart Lanterns** to help with
Health regeneration.

VOODOO CHILD

Time to hunt down a **Voodoo Demon** and catch that **Guide Voodoo Doll**. When you're ready, highlight the Guide Voodoo Doll in your Hotbar, stand near lava, and press 'T' to throw it.

Sorry, old buddy . . .

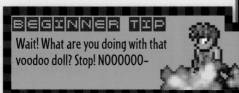
BEATING THE WALL OF FLESH

You can do this, my young friend. Don't let the Guide die in vain – especially since you're the one who killed him! Your best bet is to use a ranged weapon such as the **Molten Fury** or the **Phoenix Blaster**, as you'll want to keep a safe distance from all those sharp teeth advancing on you. Magic weapons work well too: the **Water Bolt** will do wonders here, as long as you have some **Mana Potions** handy. If you're more the yo-yo type, make sure to get yourself a **Cascade**.

It's not just a wall of flesh . . . it's a wall of teeth, too!

The Wall of Flesh will move towards you at a steady pace. Whatever you do, don't let it catch up! If it does, it will throw you ahead, causing massive damage.

Also, if you were thinking of fleeing the battle using a **Magic Mirror**, don't. You'll die a horrible death.

DEALING WITH THE HUNGRY

Your first priority is to deal with those snapping, toothy things the Wall of Flesh keeps on a leash. They're called the **Hungry**, and if you deal out enough damage to them they'll detach and go after you. Fortunately, they often drop **Hearts** when they die.

One of the Hungry off its leash

BEATING THE MOUTH AND EYES

The Wall of Flesh's **Mouth** and **Eyes** share Health, so hit any one of them to damage the whole Wall. Make sure to dodge the eyes' lasers too. The Mouth will occasionally burp **Leeches**. These don't have much Health, but they drop a **Heart** every time, making them quite useful in a pinch.

Leeches circling their prey

SURVIVAL TIP

Having a hard time staying alive? Build me a house along your path in a place where you tend to die! Talk to me and I'll throw you some Health when you need it most. Oh, and don't worry about me: I can take care of myself.

CONGRATULATIONS! YOU JUST UNLOCKED HARDMODE!

Whew! That was quite a fight, wasn't it? The Wall of Flesh just left behind a box holding your very first Hardmode treasure. Go ahead – treat yourself! You deserve a pat on the back for beating the toughest boss before Hardmode!

You'll want to grab that **Pwnhammer**, the key to creating all-new Hardmode ores. There's a chance the Wall of Flesh will also drop the **Breaker Blade**, the **Clockwork Assault Rifle**, the **Laser Rifle**, or an **Emblem** that will boost your damage depending on the type.

If you defeated the Wall of Flesh on Expert difficulty, check out its **Treasure Bag** for a **Demon Heart**, which will give you an extra equipment slot on Expert-difficulty worlds.

If you don't get the items you want, it's worth coming back down to the Underworld to kill the Wall of Flesh again once the Guide returns. But first . . . it's time for Hardmode!

CHAPTER FOUR: SURVIVING HARDMODE

HARDMODE IS NOT SO BA- AHHH!!! LOOK OUT!

Welcome to Hardmode! Your world is once again a dangerous place. Follow my instructions and I'll make sure you don't die . . . much.

THE CONSEQUENCES OF HARDMODE

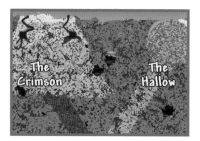

The moment you beat the Wall of Flesh, you release the ancient spirits of light and dark across the world. This means you've unleashed two diagonal bands across your map: the **Corruption** or the **Crimson** (depending on your world), and a new light-themed biome, the **Hallow**.

Everything these two lines touch above the Underworld is now extremely dangerous, and you should approach with total caution. These biomes will spread too, and will take over your other biomes as time passes.

A Floating Island caught in the Crimson crossfire

RETURN OF THE LIVING DEAD

Corrupted biomes aren't your only problem, either. Remember how scary the zombies were on your first night? Well, they found some new Hardmode friends to tear you apart if you don't get home by nightfall. Best to stick to the Underground during the night.

Aaa-oo! Werewolves now show up during the full moon.

GENERATING NEW ORES

Cheer up! Hardmode's not all bad! As a matter of fact, it's time to get started on one of the best things about Hardmode: the shiny new ores.

BACK TO THE ALTAR

Remember in Chapter Two when I suggested you spot the Evil Altars on your world? (Psst! If you've forgotten, it's on page 27.) It's time to mount a little expedition!

Here goes nothing!

The journey will be perilous, so set out at dawn and proceed with caution. The Corruption and the Crimson feature all-new baddies that will make your life difficult, but don't give up!

BLESS YOU!

Once you reach the altars, pull out your **Pwnhammer** and get smashing! Don't think of using any other hammer, by the way . . . You'll just hurt yourself.

Each Evil Altar you break with the Pwnhammer will bless your world with Hardmode ore. The first one will create either **Cobalt** or **Palladium**, the second **Mythril** or **Orichalcum**, and the third one either **Adamantite** or **Titanium**.

UH-OH . . .

Smashing altars sounds too good to be true, doesn't it? Well, there's a downside too.

Each time you destroy an Evil Altar, one or two **Wraiths** will come flying through blocks to get you. You'll also help spread corruption around your world, as each altar you destroy has a chance of creating a new block of Corruption, Crimson or Hallow somewhere. These will spread to nearby biomes and, left unchecked, will eventually take over.

MINING HARDMODE ORES

Smash as many altars as you can (I recommend around twelve, if you can find them), then get back home. Time to reap your rewards!

MINING COBALT AND PALLADIUM

Your current pickaxe won't let you mine anything other than **Cobalt** or **Palladium**, so that's what you're after for now. If you see another Hardmode ore, just place a torch next to it so you can find it easily later on.

You'll find some Cobalt or Palladium in the Underground layer, but your best bet is to head down deeper into the **Cavern**. Using a **Spelunker Potion** will make spotting new ores much easier.

Once you get enough Cobalt or Palladium, craft yourself a new pickaxe. Use any extra ore to craft yourself better weapons and armour!

RECIPE	INGREDIENTS	CRAFTING STATION
Cobalt Pickaxe (1)	Cobalt Bar (15)	
Palladium Pickaxe (1)	Palladium Bar (18)	Iron/Lead Anvil

MINING MYTHRIL AND ORICHALCUM

Once you can mine **Mythril** or **Orichalcum** ores, your next order of business is to craft yourself a **Mythril Anvil** or an **Orichalcum Anvil**. This powerful new crafting station will let you create many great Hardmode-only items.

RECIPE	INGREDIENTS	CRAFTING STATION
Mythril Anvil (1)	Mythril Bar (10)	🛠 🛠
Orichalcum Anvil (1)	Orichalcum Bar (12)	Iron/Lead Anvil

UPGRADING YOUR WEAPONS

Now that you have some good Hardmode equipment, it's time to get yourself a powerful new weapon. Here are three great choices:

RETURN TO SENDER: YO-YOS

Yo-yos continue to be all the rage in Hardmode. The **Skeleton Merchant** sells two good Hardmode yo-yos – **Format:C** and **Gradient**. Make sure to pick up some of his excellent yo-yo  accessories as well: the **Yo-yo Glove** and one of his **Counterweights**.

Another great yo-yo you can craft is the **Chik**. You can get the **Crystal Shards** and **Souls of Light** from the Underground Hallow.

RECIPE	INGREDIENTS	CRAFTING STATION
Chik (1)	Wooden Yo-yo (1) Crystal Shard (15) Soul of Light (10)	Mythril/Orichalcum Anvil

ASSAULT AND BATTERY: CLOCKWORK ASSAULT RIFLE

A great ranged weapon for early Hardmode is the Clockwork Assault Rifle, a gun that fires bullets in three-round bursts. The Wall of Flesh drops this weapon, so beat it until you get lucky. Just make sure to apologize to the Guide for sacrificing him over and over again . . .

PEW PEW: LASER RIFLE AND GOLDEN SHOWER

This great magic weapon shoots lasers that can punch through enemies. Just like the Clockwork Assault Rifle, you can get this one from the Wall of Flesh.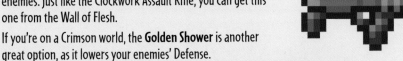

If you're on a Crimson world, the **Golden Shower** is another great option, as it lowers your enemies' Defense.

RECIPE	INGREDIENTS	CRAFTING STATION
Golden Shower (1)	Spell Tome (1) Ichor (20) Soul of Night (15)	Bookcase

GETTING YOUR WINGS

Wings are a must-have in Hardmode. Each Wings item lets you fly for a limited time when holding the spacebar, and protects you against fall damage.

I can fly!

CRAFTING WINGS

There are thirty-six different Wings in Terraria, and many of them can be crafted. Of those you can make yourself, almost all of them require one special ingredient: **Souls of Flight**. To get them, make your way to the **Space** layer and fight **Wyverns**.

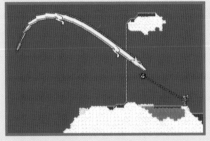

The Dao of Pow is an excellent weapon against Wyverns.

MAIDEN FLIGHT

Of all the Wings in the game, the easiest to craft early on are the **Angel Wings** or **Demon Wings**. You can get the **Souls of Light** from the Underground Hallow, and the **Souls of Night** from the Underground Corruption or Crimson.

RECIPE	INGREDIENTS	CRAFTING STATION
Angel Wings (1)	Soul of Flight (20), Feather (10) Soul of Light (25)	Mythril/Orichalcum Anvil
Demon Wings (1)	Soul of Flight (20), Feather (10) Soul of Night (25)	

Check out vendors and bosses for key ingredients to other Wing types. You can even get a set of Wings from fishing quests or Expert Mode Treasure Bags!

Lazure's Barrier Platform: a Wings-like rare drop from Expert Mode Treasure Bags

CHAPTER FIVE: HARDMODE ALLIES

FRIENDS IN HARD PLACES

Cheer up, you're not alone! Time to meet your seven new allies.

By now you should have fifteen pre-Hardmode allies helping you. But did you know you have seven further allies waiting to move in once Hardmode begins? It's true! And I'm one of them!

Make sure you build enough houses to host every one of us, and check out the next pages to find out how to befriend us.

HARDMODE ALLY CHECKLIST

FOUND?	ALLY NICKNAME	SERVICES
	The Pirate	Sells pirate-related items.
	The Truffle	Sells Autohammer and mushroom-related items.
	The Wizard	Sells magical items.
	The Steampunker	Sells Clentaminator, teleporter and other technology items.
	The Cyborg	Sells advanced explosive weapons.
	Santa Claus	Sells Christmas items.
	The Tax Collector	Collects taxes from other allies.

BEGINNER TIP

Do you have all of the pre-Hardmode allies? You'll know you do if the **Party Girl** has moved in. If you're missing any, check out **Chapter Seven** of *Terraria: The Ultimate Survival Handbook*.

MEET YOUR NEW NEIGHBOURS

Your Terraria family is growing! Here are the newcomers.

> Hands off me booty, ya scallywag!

THE PIRATE

Ahoy, me hearties! I'm the Pirate, and I'll be sellin' you some fine pirate booty! Now, smartly, matey! Fetch me a draught o' grog before Davy Jones comes a-callin'!

WHERE TO FIND ME

Arrr! I'll be movin' in to a free house as soon as ye blow down those scallywag **pirates**! Beat back a **Pirate Invasion** once and I'll share me plunder and call you 'Bucko'!

MY SERVICES

I'll be sellin' many pirate items plundered from the finest prizes on the Seven Seas! Come to me for a **cannon** and **cannonballs**, or to buy a **pirate costume**! And, once ye send a Mechanical Boss to the bottom, I'll be sellin' you the mighty **Bunny Cannon** as well. Shiver me timbers, it fires **bunnies**!

TERRARIA GOSSIP

Don't you think the Pirate looks an awful lot like the **Pirate Captain** of the Pirate Invasion? Perhaps his crew mutinied and made him walk the plank!

You haven't seen any pigs around here have you? My brother lost his leg to one.

THE TRUFFLE

Hi there! Before you stuff me into a cauldron or use me to flavour your pasta, hear me out! I know what you did with all those Glowing Mushrooms, but build me a house and we'll call it even, all right?

WHERE TO FIND ME

Getting me to move in is going to be a little bit tricky. You'll need to create a **Surface Mushroom biome** and build me a nice little house there. Call it compensation for turning all my children into Healing Potions!

MY SERVICES

Besides the **Mushroom Cap**, a Vanity hat, and the cute **Baby Truffle** that you can summon using the **Strange Glowing Mushroom**, I also sell the mighty **Mushroom Spear** and the powerful hammer known as **Hammush** – you just have to beat one of the Mechanical Bosses first. Defeat Plantera and I'll even sell you the **Autohammer**!

Finally, if you get the **Clentaminator** from the Steampunker, I can set you up with some **Dark Blue Solution** that will turn Jungle Grass into **Mushroom Grass**.

BUILDING A SURFACE MUSHROOM BIOME

Wondering how to convince the Truffle to move in? It doesn't take a wizard to figure it out! It helps to have one around to set you on the right path, though.

STEP ONE: GATHER MUSHROOM SEEDS

To get started, find an **Underground Mushroom biome** and slash those Glowing Mushrooms until you get three or four **Mushroom Grass Seeds**. (Don't worry, I won't tell the Truffle on you.)

Sorry, kiddos!

STEP TWO: LAY DOWN MUD BLOCKS

Collect at least 100 **Mud Blocks** and lay them down side by side where you want to create your new biome. Better put down 150, just to be sure.

STEP THREE: PLANT MUSHROOMS

Put down those **Mushroom Grass Seeds** and space them a little apart. Then just let time take its course!

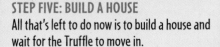

STEP FOUR: WATCH THE MUSHROOMS GROW

After a few days, **Glowing Mushrooms** will grow on your land and the sky will become dark even during the day. That's how you'll know you've made it!

STEP FIVE: BUILD A HOUSE

All that's left to do now is to build a house and wait for the Truffle to move in.

Sorry I turned your uncle into a table . . .

THE WIZARD

Hello there! Who are you again? Oh, I'm supposed to introduce myself, am I? Oh, yes, yes, of course! As you already know by now, I am a great and powerful wizard! Remember Merlin from the legend of King Arthur? Well, he came last in my wizarding class. Gurglin' Merlin, we used to call him.

WHERE TO FIND ME

You'll run into me somewhere in the Cavern layer, with my hands and feet bound. As to how I got into that situation . . . All you need to know is that was a glorious magic trick and it went wrong at the worst possible time.

My hero!

Want me to pull a coin from behind your ear? No? OK.

MY SERVICES

Once you set me free, I'll move in to an available house and sell you items of great magical power, including three magical weapons: the **Ice Rod**, the **Spell Tome** and the **harp**. I also sell **Greater Mana Potions** and a crafting station called the **crystal ball**.

THE STEAMPUNKER

Howdy, big bug! Steampunker, that's my moniker. If a thing's got gears and is made of brass, then I'm the lady for the task! I love all contraptions of the clockwork persuasion, and I've never met an engine that couldn't be made better with a few extra cogs!

WHERE TO FIND ME

I'll lodge in one of your houses once you soundly defeat a Mechanical Boss. Don't matter which one - the **Destroyer**, the **Twins** and **Skeletron Prime** all have intriguing brass I'm keen to put under a magnifying glass!

MY SERVICES

I've got all sorts of gadgets to hawk for a reasonable price. Come have a gander! Among my fine wares is the **Clentaminator**, a unique device that can transform a biome in a jiffy.

Corruption be gone!

I also provide **cogs**, **teleporters** and **jetpacks**, as well as an array of crafting stations: the **Blend-O-Matic**, the **Steampunk Boiler** and, on Crimson worlds, the **Flesh Cloning Vat**. Alight upon **Chapter Six: Hardmode Crafting** for details!

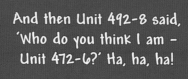
And then Unit 492-8 said,
'Who do you think I am –
Unit 472-6?' Ha, ha, ha!

THE CYBORG

Greetings, adventuring unit. I am the Cyborg, half ally, half machine. My heart might be made from carbon nanosteel, but I still love one thing: hi-tech explosives!

WHERE TO FIND ME

You'll need to exterminate the biological threat known as **Plantera** before I relocate my base of operations to one of your houses.

MY SERVICES

Since Plantera drops the **Grenade Launcher**, it is only logical that I should sell you some **rockets** to fire with it. The types of rockets I sell depend on a number of variables.

ROCKET TYPE	AVAILABLE WHEN:	DETAILS
Rocket I	Always	Small blast radius
Rocket II	Blood Moon	Small blast radius, destroys blocks
Rocket III	Night	Large blast radius
Rocket IV	Solar eclipse	Large blast radius, destroys blocks

Besides rockets, I also supply the **Proximity Mine Launcher** as well as **Nanites**, which you can use to craft items that will confuse your enemies. Hey, nanotechnology is confusing!

RECIPE	INGREDIENTS	CRAFTING STATION
Flask of Nanites (1)	Bottled Water (1) Nanites (5)	Imbuing Station
Nano Bullet (50)	Empty Bullet (50) Nanites (1)	Work Bench

SANTA CLAUS

Ho, ho, ho! Yes, child, it is me, jolly Santa Claus! Have you been naughty or nice this year? Never mind, I already know. I'm here to bring cheer to your base around the festive season!

WHERE TO FIND ME

If you want me to move in to an available house, you'll first need to defeat the **Frost Legion**. For details, flip ahead to page 63.

I'll only hang around between 15 and 31 December, though. I have an elf factory to manage the rest of the year!

Oh Christmas tree, oh Christmas tree!

MY SERVICES

Besides a Vanity **Santa suit**, I also sell a **Christmas tree** that you can decorate with **toppers**, **garlands**, **bulbs** and **lights**. What's that? You thought I was going to give those away for free? Ho, ho, ho, don't be a Scrooge!

I look pretty good for my age, right?

Bah! Here, take your shillings
and get out of my sight!

THE TAX COLLECTOR

What do you want? Can't you see I'm busy? Oh, fine, I'll introduce myself. I am the Tax Collector, which explains why the other allies around here look at me like I eat puppies for breakfast. It's about time those freeloaders paid for their housing, though, don't you think?

WHERE TO FIND ME

I'll first appear as a **Tortured Soul** in the Underworld, though how I could possibly have landed there is anyone's guess. Is it so wrong to love money more than people?

Anyway, throw some **Purification Powder** at me and I'll turn back into my usual cheerful self and move in to one of your available houses. You can buy the powder from the **Dryad**.

MY SERVICES

I'll collect taxes from all of your allies while you're off on your glorious adventures. For each in-game hour, I'll charge each of your friends - myself included - the sum of 50 Copper, up to a total of 10 Gold. Talk to me whenever you want to collect these funds. Just skip the small talk, all right? I have ledgers to balance.

CHAPTER SIX: HARDMODE CRAFTING

CRAFTING STATIONS AND MATERIALS

There are a lot of exciting new crafting options in Hardmode. Let's check them out!

HARDMODE CRAFTING STATIONS

Hardmode gives you eleven exciting new crafting stations to play with, including my very own, the **crystal ball**. Two are upgrades to your existing stations, but all offer brand-new crafting possibilities.

UPGRADES

Mythril or Orichalcum Anvil

Adamantite or Titanium Forge

THEMED FURNITURE

Steampunk Boiler

Flesh Cloning Vat*

Lihzahrd Furnace

GENERAL STATIONS

Bookcase

Crystal Ball

Autohammer

Ancient Manipulator

SPECIALIZED CRAFTS

Blend-O-Matic

Meat Grinder*

*Only available in Crimson worlds

HARDER THAN STEEL: HARDMODE ANVILS

The **Mythril** or **Orichalcum Anvil** should be your first Hardmode crafting station. Not only does it replace your old, busted anvil, but you can also craft all sorts of new and exciting weapons and armour with it. The type of anvil you should craft depends on the materials available in your world. Besides their appearance, the two are identical.

RECIPE	INGREDIENTS	CRAFTING STATION
Mythril Anvil (1)	Mythril Bar (10)	Iron/Lead Anvil
Orichalcum Anvil (1)	Orichalcum Bar (12)	

FORGED IN FIRE: HARDMODE FORGES

The **forges** are an upgraded version of the Furnace and Hellforge. Just like these pre-Hardmode stations, the purpose of the forges is to turn ores into bars. You can use them to forge Adamantite, Chlorophyte, Titanium and Spectre Bars, as well as create Crystal Blocks.

RECIPE	INGREDIENTS	CRAFTING STATION
Adamantite Forge (1)	Adamantite Ore (30) Hellforge (1)	Mythril/Orichalcum Anvil
Titanium Forge (1)	Titanium Ore (30) Hellforge (1)	

WELL READ: THE BOOKCASE

You might already be familiar with bookcases, since you can craft this piece of furniture long before Hardmode. Once Hardmode starts, though, you can use it to craft three powerful magic weapons: the **Crystal Storm**, the **Cursed Flames** and the **Golden Shower**. You'll need a **Spell Tome** for all three. Good thing I sell them!

RECIPE	INGREDIENTS	CRAFTING STATION
Crystal Storm (1)	Crystal Shard (20) Soul of Light (15) Spell Tome (1)	
Cursed Flames (1)	Cursed Flame (20) Soul of Night (15) Spell Tome (1)	Bookcase
Golden Shower (1)	Ichor (20) Soul of Night (15) Spell Tome (1)	

Any bookcase, no matter the style, can be used as a crafting station. You can even pick up a **Dungeon Bookcase** or an **Obsidian Bookcase** if you're too lazy to craft one yourself.

RECIPE	INGREDIENTS	CRAFTING STATION
Bookcase (1)	Wood (20) Book (10)	Sawmill

CRAFTING TIP

Did you know that there are no fewer than thirty-two different types of bookcase in Terraria? To learn more about furniture styles, check out the Furniture Guide on page 63 in *Terraria: Crafting and Construction Handbook*.

CRYSTAL CLEAR: THE CRYSTAL BALL

Time to talk about the most magical crafting station of all: the crystal ball!

With the crystal ball, you can create a great number of animated decorative blocks, such as **Waterfall Blocks**, **Magic Lava Droppers**, **Living Fire Blocks** and **Confetti Blocks**.

Most useful of all are the **Endless Quiver** and the **Endless Musket Pouch**, which give you an infinite supply of arrows or musket balls!

RECIPE	INGREDIENTS	CRAFTING STATION
Endless Quiver (1)	Wooden Arrow (3996)	Crystal Ball
Endless Musket Pouch (1)	Musket Ball (3996)	

But that's not all! You can also **right-click** on the crystal ball to get a boost to your magic stats, including maximum mana, magic damage, critical hit chance and reduced mana usage.

All this for 10 Gold, from your friend the Wizard! Get yours today! Tell your friends!

CRYSTAL BALL AND LIQUIDS

Some items, such as the Waterfall Block and the Magic Droppers, require a liquid close by to craft them. For this reason, it's best to place **water**, **lava** and **honey** right next to your crystal ball.

Water, lava and honey – all within easy reach

HAMMER TIME: THE AUTOHAMMER

The Autohammer lets you turn **Chlorophyte Bars** into **Shroomite Bars**. These mushroom-infused bars are the main ingredient of the **Shroomite Armor** set, the armour of choice if you prefer ranged attacks.

RECIPE	INGREDIENTS	CRAFTING STATION
Shroomite Bar (1)	Chlorophyte Bar (1) Glowing Mushroom (1)	Autohammer

Besides armour, you can also use Shroomite Bars to craft a unique flying item called the **Hoverboard**, as well as the super-fast **Shroomite Digging Claw**. You can buy the Autohammer from the Truffle after you defeat Plantera.

LUNAR MAGIC: THE ANCIENT MANIPULATOR

Get ready for the ultimate crafting! This crafting station is only available once you beat the **Lunatic Cultist**, and it lets you turn **Fragments** and **Luminite** into the most powerful items, armour and weapons available in Terraria.

To learn all about the Lunatic Cultist, flip ahead to **Chapter Eleven: The Moon Lord** on page 76!

ROAD RUNNER: THE BLEND-O-MATIC

The Blend-O-Matic produces one item only, but it's a good one: **Asphalt Blocks**. After three

seconds running on them, your speed will more than triple. This makes Asphalt a great building block for boss arenas or your Sky Bridge! You can buy this station from the Steampunker.

Prepare for ludicrous speed!

RECIPE	INGREDIENTS	CRAFTING STATION
Asphalt Block (1)	Stone Block (2) Gel (1)	Blend-O-Matic

NICE TO MEAT YOU: THE MEAT GRINDER

This grisly item lets you turn **Crimstone Blocks** into **Flesh Blocks**. You can use these as macabre walls, or turn them into spooky furniture using the **Flesh Cloning Vat**.

The Meat Grinder can only be found on Crimson worlds. You can get it from **Herplings**, **Crimslimes**, **Floaty Grosses** and **Crimson Axes** in your world's Crimson biome.

RECIPE	INGREDIENTS	CRAFTING STATION
Flesh Block (1)	Crimstone Block (2)	Meat Grinder

HARDMODE STYLE: FURNITURE STATIONS

Hardmode offers you two new ways to personalize your furniture with the **Steampunk Boiler** and the **Lihzahrd Furnace**. If you're on a Crimson world, you'll also get the **Flesh Cloning Vat**.

You can buy the Steampunk Boiler from the **Steampunker** for 10 Gold. You'll need **cogs** to craft furniture, and the Steampunker sells them for 7 Silver.

The Steampunker also sells the Flesh Cloning Vat for 10 Gold, though she'll only have it in stock in Crimson worlds. You'll need the **Meat Grinder** and a supply of **Crimstone Blocks** to create the **Flesh Blocks** used to craft these pieces of furniture.

Finally, you'll find the Lihzahrd Furnace in the **Lihzahrd Chests** of the Jungle Temple. This crafting station uses **Lihzahrd Bricks**, which require a **Picksaw** or better to mine. Since you get the Picksaw by defeating Golem, it's nearly impossible to use the Lihzahrd Furnace before you've mastered the Jungle Temple.

Steampunk, Flesh and Lihzahrd Bookcases

HARDMODE MINING TOOLS

All pickaxes in Hardmode can mine every single block from pre-Hardmode, so don't worry about leaving your trusty **Molten Pickaxe** or **Reaver Shark** behind.

PICKAXE/DRILL TYPE	RECIPE	CRAFTING STATION	CAN MINE...
Cobalt	Cobalt Bar (15)	Lead/Iron Anvil	Cobalt Palladium Mythril Orichalcum
Palladium	Palladium Bar (18)		
Mythril	Mythril Bar (15)	Mythril/Orichalcum Anvil	Cobalt Palladium Mythril Orichalcum Adamantite Titanium
Orichalcum	Orichalcum Bar (18)		
Adamantite	Adamantite Bar (18)		
Titanium	Titanium Bar (20)		
Pickaxe Axe* Drax*	Hallowed Bar (18), Soul of Might (1) Soul of Sight (1), Soul of Fright (1)		All except Lihzahrd Brick
Chlorophyte	Chlorophyte Bar (18)		
Shroomite Digging Claw*	Shroomite Bar (18)		
Spectre	Spectre Bar (18)		
Picksaw*	*Dropped by Golem*	Ancient Manipulator	All blocks
Solar Flare	Solar Fragment (12), Luminite Bar (10)		
Vortex	Vortex Fragment (12), Luminite Bar (10)		
Nebula	Nebula Fragment (12) Luminite Bar (10)		
Stardust	Stardust Fragment (12), Luminite Bar (10)		
Laser Drill*	*Dropped by Flying Saucer during Martian Madness event*		
Drill Containment Unit	Luminite Bar (40), Chlorophyte Bar (40) Shroomite Bar (40), Spectre Bar (40) Hellstone Bar (40), Meteorite Bar (40)	Mythril/Orichalcum Anvil	

* Also works as an axe

STYLE TIP

Did you notice you now have the choice to craft either a **pickaxe** or a **drill** for most of the pickaxe types? There's very little difference between the two, so just pick the one you think looks cooler!

SPECIAL METALS

You already know how to create Hardmode ores by smashing altars with your Pwnhammer, but what about the other Hardmode bars? Here's the rundown.

SPOOKY STUFF: SPECTRE BARS

Spectre Bars let you craft the powerful **Spectre Armor**, a set that boosts your magic attacks. Besides Chlorophyte, you also need **Ectoplasm** to craft Spectre Bars; you can get it from **Dungeon Spirits** in the Dungeon once you've defeated Plantera.

Facing off against a Dungeon Spirit

RECIPE	INGREDIENTS	CRAFTING STATION
Spectre Bar (2)	Chlorophyte Bar (2) Ectoplasm (1)	Titanium/Adamantite Forge

PAINTING TIP

You can also use Spectre Bars to craft the ultimate painting tools: the **Spectre Paintbrush**, the **Spectre Paint Roller** and the **Spectre Paint Scraper**. You'll need twenty-four Spectre Bars to craft the whole set.

HOLY METAL: HALLOWED BAR

These bars drop when you defeat any of the **Mechanical Bosses**. You can use them to craft weapons and armour that will help you to survive the perils of the Underground Jungle.

GREEN MINING: CHLOROPHYTE ORE

Chlorophyte Ore grows in the Underground Jungle once you enter Hardmode, but you need the **Pickaxe Axe** or better to mine it. That means you'll need to beat one of the **Mechanical Bosses** to get Hallowed Bars first. Not only can you use Clorophyte Ore to craft better weapons, tools and armour, but it's also a component in **Spectre Bars** and **Shroomite Bars**. Mine plenty of it to get ready for Plantera!

MOON GLOW: LUMINITE

To collect the elusive Luminite, you'll need to face the ultimate challenge: the Moon Lord himself! Luminite Bars are required to craft many of the most powerful weapons, armour and tools in Terraria. Flip ahead to page 76 of **Chapter Eleven: The Moon Lord** to learn how to defeat the Moon Lord!

RECIPE	INGREDIENTS	CRAFTING STATION
Luminite Bar (1)	Luminite (4)	Ancient Manipulator

THE ULTIMATE DRILL

There's a good reason to keep those extra bars you collect throughout Hardmode: they're an ingredient for the ultimate drill, the **Drill Containment Unit!**

This unique mining item is not your standard-issue pickaxe; instead, it's a Mount item that you equip in your **Special Equipment** menu. By summoning the **Drill Mount**, you can mine every single block in the game at amazing speed. It's also a flying mount, which means you can fly around for as long as you like.

Flying around with the Drill Mount

An area cleared out with the Drill Mount

The Drill Containment Unit is the ultimate tool if you want to clear out entire areas in a matter of seconds. The Drill Mount's lasers can blast blocks of up to ten tiles.

What's the catch, you ask? Well, there is one: the Drill Containment Unit is crazy expensive! You'll need six different bars to craft it, including **Luminite Bars**, which are only available from the Moon Lord himself. The Drill Containment Unit is the ultimate mining prize!

RECIPE	INGREDIENTS	CRAFTING STATION
Drill Containment Unit (1)	Luminite Bar (40) Chlorophyte Bar (40) Shroomite Bar (40) Spectre Bar (40) Hellstone Bar (40) Meteorite Bar (40)	Mythril/Orichalcum Anvil

CHAPTER SEVEN: HARDMODE BOSSES

TAKE DOWN THE TOP MONSTERS

Grab your weapons. We're going boss hunting!

THE DESTROYER

Say hello to the Eater of Worlds 2.0! Just like his predecessor, the Destroyer is a giant worm that can attack through blocks.

SUMMON HIM

The Destroyer can sometimes appear on his own, but otherwise you'll need to use a **Mechanical Worm** at night to summon him.

RECIPE	INGREDIENTS	CRAFTING STATION
Mechanical Worm (1)	Rotten Chunk* (6), Iron/Lead Bar (5), Soul of Night (6)	Mythril/Orichalcum Anvil

* Replaced by Vertebrae on Crimson worlds

BEAT HIM

Just like with the Eater of Worlds, piercing weapons that hit multiple body parts really are a must here. Depending on your fighting style, you can consider yo-yos or the **cutlass** for melee, the **Clockwork Assault Rifle** for ranged, and the **Laser Rifle** or **Golden Shower**. Regardless of your fighting style, you can also use the **Nimbus Rod** to boost your overall damage. Finally, using a **Bewitching Table** and the **Spider Staff** to summon spiders will help give you an edge.

Just make sure to dodge the Destroyer's attacks, which include lasers, and destroy the **probes** he launches for extra Hearts in the heat of battle.

LOOT HIM

The Destroyer drops **Souls of Might**, **Hallowed Bars** and some **Greater Healing Potions**. One great item you can craft with Souls of Might is the **Megashark**, which should help you with some of the other bosses.

RECIPE	INGREDIENTS	CRAFTING STATION
Megashark (1)	Soul of Might (20), Shark Fin (5) Illegal Gun Parts (1), Minishark (1)	Mythril/Orichalcum Anvil

THE TWINS

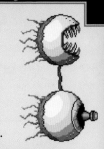

These bug-eyed monstrosities are an upgraded version of the **Eye of Cthulhu,** and are the second Mechanical Boss.

SUMMON THEM

The Twins can appear on their own when you destroy an Evil Altar, but summoning them yourself using a **Mechanical Eye** at night is more reliable.

RECIPE	INGREDIENTS	CRAFTING STATION
Mechanical Eye (1)	Lens (3), Iron/Lead Bar (5) Soul of Light (6)	Mythril/Orichalcum Anvil

BEAT THEM

The red-eyed **Retinazer** fires lasers at you, while the green-eyed **Spazmatism** shoots **Cursed Flames.** Much like the Eye of Cthulhu, they both fire at you for a while, then charge at high speed. You can fight them on your Sky Bridge, so that you can run away and see their charge attacks coming while you shoot at them with ranged weapons.

After you deal enough damage, they'll change and become even deadlier. It's best to kill Spazmatism first; once it's down, turn your attention to the remaining sibling!

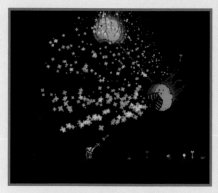

Spazmatism in its second phase

LOOT THEM

The Twins drop **Hallowed Bars, Greater Healing Potions** and **Souls of Sight.** One great item to craft with them is the **Optic Staff,** which will give you an edge against the Destroyer and Skeletron Prime.

RECIPE	INGREDIENTS	CRAFTING STATION
Optic Staff (1)	Black Lens (1), Lens (2) Hallowed Bar (12), Soul of Sight (20)	Mythril/Orichalcum Anvil

SKELETRON PRIME

The third Mechanical Boss, Skeletron Prime brings some seriously deadly hardware to a hectic fight. Skeletron Prime is considered by many as the easiest of the Mechanical Bosses, so try him first if you're not sure where to start.

SUMMON HIM

Just like the other Mechanical Bosses, Skeletron Prime can appear on his own in Hardmode, but it's best to summon him using the **Mechanical Skull**.

RECIPE	INGREDIENTS	CRAFTING STATION
Mechanical Skull (1)	Bone (30) Iron/Lead Bar (5) Soul of Light (3) Soul of Night (3)	Mythril/Orichalcum Anvil

BEAT HIM

Skeletron Prime can use four different weapons at the same time: a bomb-firing **cannon**, a **laser**, a **saw** and a **vice**. Take out at least two limbs before dealing with the head, and all four if possible, as this significantly weakens Skeletron Prime. Make sure to dodge the saw, as it hits hard, and leave the head alone while it's spinning – it deals out high damage in this state and has increased defence.

Skeletron Prime's weapons: cannon, laser, saw and vice

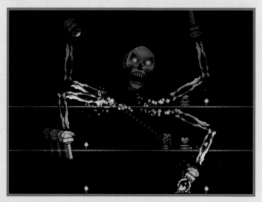

Skeletron Prime's attack

The grenades from the Prime Cannon can be a problem, as they explode on contact with blocks. Build an arena out of Wooden Platforms and the grenades will just fall through.

LOOT HIM

Besides **Souls of Fright**, Skeletron Prime also drops **Hallowed Bars** and **Greater Healing Potions**.

PLANTERA

This nasty flower, by any other name, would still bite your head off! Make sure you have a full set of **Chlorophyte Armor** and weapons before you try to uproot it.

SUMMON IT

The only way to summon Plantera is to locate **Plantera's Bulb** in the Underground Jungle. Just break it with a pickaxe or drill and Plantera will come. Get ready for a fight!

BEAT IT

Build a new battle arena in the Underground Jungle, then have Plantera follow you there before starting the fight. Whatever you do, don't leave the Underground Jungle or Plantera will become enraged!

You can defeat Plantera by dodging its attacks and hitting the central bulb. Once you bring it down to half its Health, Plantera will expose its leafy teeth and attack faster. Be sure to dodge the hooks, but you don't have to destroy them, only the head.

Plantera's Bulb

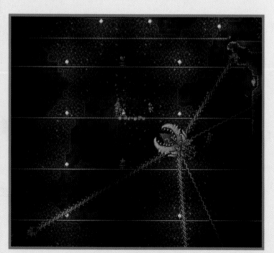

Plantera's second form

LOOT IT

Plantera drops the **Temple Key**, which lets you enter the **Jungle Temple** and face **Golem**. You'll also get a **Grenade Launcher** and some **Rocket Is** the first time, and possibly a few other cool Jungle-themed weapons.

GOLEM

Meet Golem, the stone-faced idol of the Lihzahrd tribe. He'll stomp on your face if you're not careful!

SUMMON HIM

You'll need to defeat Plantera to get a **Temple Key** and enter the Jungle Temple. Once inside, bring a **Lihzahrd Power Cell** to the glowing altar in the main room and **right-click** on the **Lihzahrd Altar**. Better set up your battle arena first!

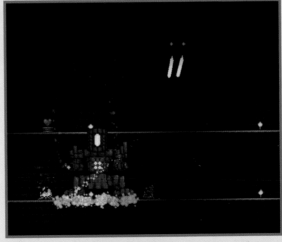

The Lihzahrd Altar

BEAT HIM

Golem will first attack by trying to stomp you and by shooting his fists at you. You can take out the fists, but the head is your main target. Damage the head enough and it will start flying around, shooting fireballs. Keep it up!

The body is your target in the second phase. Avoid its stomps and the head's fireballs and you'll win in no time.

LOOT HIM

Golem drops tons of powerful weapons, as well as the **Picksaw**, a pickaxe and saw combo powerful enough to break Lihzahrd Bricks. You'll also get **Beetle Husks**, used to craft **Beetle Armor**, the most powerful armour for melee characters prior to defeating the Moon Lord.

Golem's second form. Watch out!

DUKE FISHRON

There's always a bigger fish – unless it's Duke Fishron! You don't need to beat this powerful boss to get to the Moon Lord, but the gear he drops can make a big difference.

A Truffle Worm

SUMMON HIM

Look for a **Truffle Worm** in Underground Mushroom biomes. Once you spot one, equip your **bug net** and catch it quick! The Truffle Worm digs down to safety when you get too close. Once you catch a Truffle Worm, go to the Ocean and cast your line.

BEAT HIM

Duke Fishron is one of the toughest fights in the game as he has tons of Health and some devastating attacks. You'll have to dodge everything from sharks to deadly bubbles, but keep at it and you'll take him down!

Good luck dodging all that!

LOOT HIM

Duke Fishron drops some of the best items in the game, including the **Flairon**, the **Tsunami Bow**, the **Razorblade Typhoon**, the **Tempest Staff** and the **Bubble Gun**. They'll make a big difference against the Moon Lord.

CHAPTER EIGHT: HARDMODE EVENTS

MONSTERS, ALIENS AND CHRISTMAS TREES

The Martians are coming! And the movie monsters. And the pirates. Oh, and the Christmas elves too.

Note that many of these events are quite challenging! Consider building a dedicated arena or fighting area to take care of the multiple waves of enemies these events present. For instance, you can dig a shallow pit and fill it with a layer of lava, or upgrade your traps using those from the **Jungle Temple**.

FROST LEGION

This holiday-themed invasion requires an item that can only be found during the Christmas season, between 15 and 31 December.

START IT

You can launch the Frost Legion event by using a **Snow Globe**. Although you can use the Snow Globe all year round, you can only find it by opening **presents** dropped by monsters around Christmastime.

BEAT IT

Frost Legion event battles work pretty much the same way as fighting the Goblin Army: kill as many snowmen as you can until the bar in the bottom-right corner fills to one hundred per cent.

LOOT

The snowmen in the Frost Legion don't drop anything interesting besides **Snow Blocks** but, once you defeat the Frost Legion, **Santa Claus** will show up around the holiday season with tons of goodies for sale. Flip back to page 45 if you need a Santa refresher.

Do you want to slay a snowman?

PIRATE INVASION

Arr, matey! These gold-loving scallywags are here to send you to meet Davy Jones, so look sharp!

START IT

There's a small chance of a Pirate Invasion every morning after you've destroyed your first Evil Altar. To start the invasion on your own, fight monsters around the Ocean until one drops the **Pirate Map**.

BEAT IT

You must kill 120 pirates to defeat the invasion. Watch out for the extra-tough **Pirate Captain**, as well as the Pirate Invasion mini-boss, the **Flying Dutchman**. To defeat this flying ship, take out its four cannons.

LOOT

The Pirate Invasion is the only source of all types of **gold furniture**, from doors to candelabras and pianos. You can also get the **cutlass**, a powerful weapon in early Hardmode, as well as items that help you to win or save Gold, such as the **Lucky Coin**, the **Discount Card** and the **Gold Ring**.

Flying Dutchman attack!

SOLAR ECLIPSE

B-movie monsters are on the move! Look out for your favourite thrillers and slashers in this day-long invasion.

START IT

Solar eclipses may happen naturally when you defeat a Mechanical Boss. To trigger one of your own, collect eight **Solar Tablet Fragments** from the **Jungle Temple**. Use the **Solar Tablet** during the day to get started.

RECIPE	INGREDIENTS	CRAFTING STATION
 **Solar Tablet (1)**	Solar Tablet Fragment (8)	Mythril/Orichalcum Anvil

HELPFUL HACK

Many of the most powerful monsters – including those who drop the best treasure – only show up after you beat Plantera.

Mothron's egg is about to hatch!

BEAT IT

The solar eclipse will continue until sunset. A good base setup will protect you against most invaders, but watch out for the **Reapers**, who can fly through blocks. You'll also face a mini-boss, **Mothron**, who will lay down eggs that will hatch into **Baby Mothrons**.

LOOT

The monsters of the solar eclipse drop various useful items and weapons such as the **Nail Gun**, the **Death Sickle** and the **Deadly Sphere Staff**. Mothron sometimes drops a **Broken Hero Sword**, which you can use to craft **True Night's Edge**, **True Excalibur** and even the mystical **Terra Blade**!

MARTIAN MADNESS

The Martians are coming! Get ready for an onslaught of sci-fi critters and some great hi-tech gear.

START IT

After you defeat Golem, a **Martian Probe** will sometimes appear in the outer two-thirds of your map, especially in Space. It will turn red and flee as soon as it spots you; let it return to the mothership to get the invasion started.

BEAT IT

Bring the progress bar in the bottom-right corner of your screen to one hundred per cent to beat the Alien Invasion. Some enemies, such as the **Flying Saucer** mini-boss, are worth more than the Martian foot soldiers, but they also require more effort.

Life form detected!

Watch out for that deathray!

LOOT

All Martian invaders drop **Martian Conduit Plating**, a building component used to craft Martian-themed furniture. The **Flying Saucers** also drop many awesome weapons, such as the **Laser Machinegun** and the **Xeno Staff**, as well as the powerful **laser drill** and the **Cosmic Car Key**, which summons a **UFO Mount** that can fly indefinitely.

PUMPKIN MOON

This Halloween-themed event is a tough but fun fight. Despite its seasonal nature, you can trigger it at any time.

START IT

Launch the Pumpkin Moon by using a **Pumpkin Moon Medallion** at night. Pumpkins are more abundant around Halloween, but you can grow them at any time of the year by purchasing **Pumpkin Seeds** from the **Dryad**. You can gather **Ectoplasm** from the **Dungeon Spirits** in the Hardmode Dungeon, and the **Hallowed Bars** from the **Mechanical Bosses**.

RECIPE	INGREDIENTS	CRAFTING STATION
Pumpkin Moon Medallion (1)	Pumpkin (30), Ectoplasm (5) Hallowed Bar (10)	Mythril/Orichalcum Anvil

BEAT IT

The Pumpkin Moon event always ends at sunrise. Invaders come in waves: the higher the wave, the tougher the monsters and the better the rewards. To complete a wave, score the points indicated in the bottom-right corner; tougher monsters are worth more points. Reach Wave 15 and you'll get an Achievement: **Baleful Harvest**.

Things get hectic around Wave 15

LOOT

This event's two mini-bosses, **Mourning Wood** and **Pumpking**, drop many Halloween-themed items, including weapons, pets, hooks and Vanity items. **Splinterlings** and **Mourning Woods** also drop **Spooky Wood**, used to craft spooky-looking furniture and armour.

FROST MOON

Much like the Pumpkin Moon, the Frost Moon is a holiday-themed event that you can trigger all year round. It's an especially hard event that will push your fighting skills to the limit!

START IT

You can launch the Frost Moon by using a **Naughty Present** after sunset. Get the **Ectoplasm** from the Hardmode Dungeon and the **Souls of Fright** from Skeletron Prime.

RECIPE	INGREDIENTS	CRAFTING STATION
Naughty Present (1)	Silk (20), Ectoplasm (5) Soul of Fright (5)	Mythril/Orichalcum Anvil

BEAT IT

The Frost Moon works just like the Pumpkin Moon: the monsters come in waves, with each wave offering bigger challenges and rewards. Make it to Wave 15 for a special Achievement: **Ice Scream**. The event ends at sunrise, so don't waste a second!

Frost Moon's three mini-bosses: Santa-NK1,

LOOT

The three Frost Moon mini-bosses – **Santa-NK1**, **Ice Queen** and **Everscream** – offer excellent Christmas-themed loot, including powerful weapons such as a spear called the **North Pole**, plus two great magic weapons, the **Blizzard Staff** and **Razorpine**. You can even get a special Rudolph flying mount from the Ice Queen!

CHAPTER NINE: HARDMODE ADVENTURES

TERRARIA'S ULTIMATE SURVIVAL CHALLENGES

Hardmode has two new challenging adventures for you: the Jungle Temple and the Hardmode Dungeon. Enemies inbound!

THE JUNGLE TEMPLE

Remember that unbreakable temple you found exploring the Underground Jungle? Time to go uncover its deepest and darkest secrets!

ENTER IT

To enter, you'll need to get the **Temple Key** from **Plantera**. Once you have the key, look for the **Lihzahrd Door** located near the top of the Jungle Temple. Get ready for a challenge!

CONQUER IT

Lihzahrds and **Flying Snakes** come hard and fast in the Jungle Temple, but perhaps most dangerous of all are the various traps lying in wait. Make sure to bring a **wire cutter** with you, and equip it to see and cut the wires.

Whew! The wire cutter exposes three dangerous traps.

LOOT

The temple's main treasures are the **Lihzahrd Power Cells** used to summon Golem, and the **Solar Tablet Fragments** which you can assemble to start a **solar eclipse**. You'll have to pry the temple's best loot from the stony hands of Golem himself. (See page 61.)

COMBAT TIP
Make sure to mine a few of those deadly traps you see all over the Jungle Temple . . . They'll make a killer upgrade to your home defences!

THE HARDMODE DUNGEON

The Dungeon offers all-new deadly challenges and plenty of new treasures once you defeat Plantera.

START IT

The Dungeon doesn't enter Hardmode as soon as you beat the Wall of Flesh; instead, you'll have to wait until you beat **Plantera** before you can face this challenge.

CONQUER IT

Just like the old Dungeon of yore, the Hardmode Dungeon can get pretty hectic if you don't kill monsters quickly enough. Many of them, such as the **Necromancer** and the **Giant Cursed Skull**, can even attack you through blocks.

The rarer enemies in the Dungeon are especially deadly: monsters such as the **Paladin** or **Bone Lee** can make short work of you, so watch out!

Dodging the Paladin's hammers

LOOT

There's one great reason to visit the Hardmode Dungeon: loot! This includes many powerful items and weapons dropped by monsters, but also **Biome Chests** – special chests that can only be opened using a rare key from monsters found in the corresponding biome.

For more info about the loot you'll find in the Hardmode Dungeon, check out *Terraria: Exploration and Adventure Handbook*, on pages 66 and 67!

CHAPTER TEN: THE LUNAR EVENTS

THE ROAD TO TERRARIA'S ULTIMATE BOSS

Ready to take down the Moon Lord? You'll have to defeat these tough challenges first!

THE LUNATIC CULTIST

To trigger the Lunar Events, you'll first need to take down the **Lunatic Cultist**. To prepare, fight **Golem** and **Plantera** a few times, or try your luck with the **Martian Madness** or **Duke Fishron** until you have all the equipment you need.

SUMMON HIM

Once you defeat **Golem**, a group of cultists will appear at the entrance to the Dungeon. Kill them to catch the Lunatic Cultist's attention. Don't worry: those guys are real pushovers.

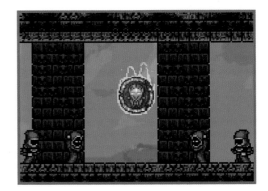

BEAT HIM

If possible, get the **Cosmic Car Key** from the Martian Event so you can take the fight to the skies. The Lunatic Cultist casts a number of spells, including making doubles of himself, but with some practice you'll learn to dodge his most devastating attacks.

LOOT HIM

The Lunatic Cultist drops one important item: the **Ancient Manipulator**. We'll use it shortly to craft some of the most powerful items in the game!

THE CELESTIAL PILLARS

Once the Lunatic Cultist is dead, four Celestial Pillars appear around your world. Kill one hundred enemies around a pillar to bring its shields down, then attack the pillar to destroy it.

THE VORTEX PILLAR

This Celestial Pillar is protected by aliens with powerful ranged attacks. Be especially careful with the **Alien Queens**, who can hit you with a stinger that can mess with your gravity. Kill any **Alien Larvae** you see before they have a chance to grow into Alien Queens.

MONSTER TYPE	ABILITIES
Vortexian	Opens portals that shoot lightning bolts
Alien Queen	Messes up your gravity
Alien Hornet	Can grow into an Alien Queen
Alien Larva	Can grow into an Alien Hornet
Storm Diver	Uses ranged attacks

VORTEX GEAR

Equipment made from **Vortex Fragments** favours ranged attacks.

For now, you can craft the **Vortex Fragments** into two powerful ranged weapons: the **Vortex Beater**, a gun that fires explosives bullets, and the **Phantasm**, an auto-fire bow that shoots four arrows at once.

RECIPE	INGREDIENTS	CRAFTING STATION
Vortex Beater (1)	Vortex Fragment (18)	Ancient Manipulator
Phantasm (1)	Vortex Fragment (18)	

THE STARDUST PILLAR

This pillar is all about summoners. The monsters here will call upon small versions of themselves to try to overpower you through sheer numbers. Even the Stardust Pillar itself can summon monsters to fight you.

MONSTER TYPE	ABILITIES
Star Cell	When it dies, it splits into smaller versions that can grow back into Star Cells
Flow Invader	Fires high-speed projectiles
Twinkle Popper	Can spawn Twinkles
Twinkle	Explodes on contact
Milkyway Weaver	Only the head is vulnerable
Stargazer	Fires a deadly laser

STARDUST GEAR

Just like the monsters of the Stardust Pillar, the items you can craft with Stardust Fragments are all about summoning minions to do your bidding.

At this point, you can use Stardust Fragments to craft two powerful summoning weapons: the **Stardust Cell Staff** summons a **Stardust Cell**, which fires mini versions of itself at enemies, while the **Stardust Dragon Staff** calls upon a deadly dragon that attacks nearby enemies. This **Stardust Dragon** grows in length with each use of the staff, up to your summon limit.

RECIPE	INGREDIENTS	CRAFTING STATION
Stardust Cell Staff (1)	Stardust Fragment (18)	Ancient Manipulator
Stardust Dragon Staff (1)	Stardust Fragment (18)	Ancient Manipulator

THE NEBULA PILLAR

The Nebula Pillar is all about magic attacks. The monsters that protect it can fire off projectiles at range, or teleport closer to inflict damage. Watch out for the **Brain Sucklers** as they latch on to your head and inflict damage while blocking your vision!

MONSTER TYPE		ABILITIES
	Nebula Floater	Can ram, teleport and shoot lasers
	Brain Suckler	Latches on to victim's head and blocks vision
	Predictor	Shoots projectiles
	Evolution Beast	Rams or shoots slow-moving spheres

NEBULA GEAR

Items crafted from **Nebula Fragments** are a magician's dream! For the moment, you can use them to create two powerful magic items: the **Nebula Arcanum** fires homing, bouncing orbs, while the **Nebula Blaze** auto-fires high-speed projectiles that can zero in on your enemies.

RECIPE	INGREDIENTS	CRAFTING STATION
Nebula Arcanum (1)	Nebula Fragment (18)	
Nebula Blaze (1)	Nebula Fragment (18)	Ancient Manipulator

THE SOLAR PILLAR

The Solar Pillar is all about close combat. Enemies here have strong defences and will try to get right up in your face at every opportunity. Best stick to the ground to avoid the Crawltipedes, and watch out for fireballs coming from the pillar itself.

MONSTER TYPE	ABILITIES
Selenian	Can reflect projectiles when it charges
Drakanian	Rides a Drakomire
Corite	Charges at high speed
Sroller	Curls into a ball and charges
Crawltipede	Invulnerable (except its tail, that is!)
Drakomire	Shoots solar flares

SOLAR GEAR

The gear crafted from **Solar Fragments** is ideal for players who like to get up close and personal with monsters. For now, you can use Solar Fragments to craft two great melee weapons: the **Solar Eruption**, which can shoot a long sword-like whip through blocks, and **Daybreak**, a javelin-style projectile weapon that sticks to enemies and damages them over time.

RECIPE	INGREDIENTS	CRAFTING STATION
Solar Eruption (1)	Solar Fragment (18)	Ancient Manipulator
Daybreak (1)	Solar Fragment (18)	

CHAPTER ELEVEN:
THE MOON LORD

TERRARIA'S ULTIMATE CHALLENGE!

It's time to take down the Moon Lord. Get ready for the fight of your life!

THE MOON LORD IS COMING!

Impending doom approaches! Time to face Terraria's biggest and baddest boss. Once you defeat the four Celestial Towers during the Lunar Events, you've got one minute to prepare for this epic fight.

EQUIPMENT

There are many ways to defeat the Moon Lord, but they all require skills and preparation. Craft a stack of each useful potion you can think of, including **Regeneration**, **Ironskin**, **Endurance** and **Heartreach Potions**, as well as two stacks of **Greater Healing** and **Greater Mana Potions**.

Get yourself a set of **Beetle Armor**, **Shroomite Armor**, or **Spectre Armor**, as well as the best weapon you can find. The **Flairon** and the **Razorblade Typhoon**, both dropped by **Duke Fishron**, are especially useful.

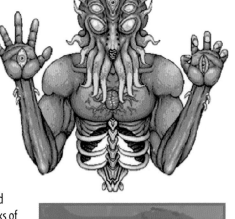

Beetle Armor and Flairon. Ready to rock!

BATTLE ARENA

Movement is crucial in this fight. Make sure there's plenty of space to jump around in your battle arena, or consider taking the fight to your **Sky Bridge**, where you'll be able to run away from the Moon Lord as you fire back at him. Position the Nurse somewhere along this bridge so you can reach her for a quick fix!

Another option is to use the **Cosmic Car Key** from the Martian Madness event. You can use it to fly around and dodge the Moon Lord's deadly attacks.

THE FIGHT

The Moon Lord throws a lot of attacks at you, and you'll have to practise in order to dodge them the best you can. The deadliest of all is the **Phantasmal Deathray**: you can tell it's coming when the Moon Lord opens his central eye.

Dodge his attacks while evenly spreading the damage between the eyes in his hands and head. Once you destroy them, they'll spawn a **True Eye of Cthulhu** that packs quite a punch, so it's better to kill them as closely together as possible.

If the Moon Lord grabs you with its tongue, it will create **Moon Leech Clots** that will heal him should they reach his mouth. Make sure to take them out fast!

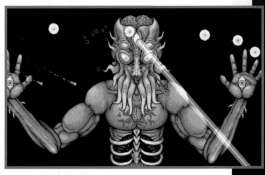

Phantasmal Deathray!

Almost ... there ...

FINISH HIM!

Once you've taken care of the Moon Lord's eyes, his chest will open up and expose his heart. Hit it with everything you've got – but don't forget to dodge!

IF AT FIRST YOU DON'T SUCCEED ...

The Moon Lord is one tough fight. Don't get discouraged if you're defeated during your first battle with him! To try again, simply kill the Lunatic Cultist for a second time, or, if you have extra Fragments lying around, craft a **Celestial Sigil** to summon the Moon Lord directly. Upgrade your equipment and have another go!

RECIPE	INGREDIENTS	CRAFTING STATION
Celestial Sigil (1)	Solar Fragment (20), Vortex Fragment (20) Nebula Fragment (20), Stardust Fragment (20)	Ancient Manipulator

A HERO'S REWARD

You did it! You beat the Moon Lord! Go ahead, celebrate! Jump around, do a little jig! You earned it!

When you're done dancing, be sure to pick up your loot, which contains some of the very best items in Terraria.

Fun with portals

The Moon Lord drops a **Portal Gun**, which you can use to create linked portals with the left and right mouse buttons. You'll also get 70 to 90 **Luminite**, which you can turn into **Luminite Bars** to craft the best armour, weapons and wings in the game.

Finally, you'll also get one of the following weapons:

ITEM	DESCRIPTION
Meowmere	Fires cat-shaped projectiles
Terrarian	Fires projectiles at enemies
Star Wrath	Projectiles fall at cursor
S.D.M.G. (Space Dolphin Machine Gun)	Fast-firing gun
Celebration	Fires two rockets at once
Last Prism	Fires beams of light
Lunar Flare	Summons magic projectiles
Rainbow Crystal Staff	Summons crystal sentry
Lunar Portal Staff	Summons portal that fires at enemies

Didn't get the weapon you wanted? Time to summon the Moon Lord again!